SUNRISE SUMMITS

A POETRY ANTHOLOGY

Edited by
DEAN K MILLER

Copyright © 2020
All rights reserved. This book or any portion thereof may not be reproduced or used in any manner whatsoever without the express written permission of the publisher except for the use of brief quotations in a book review.

Printed in the United States of America
First Printing, 2016
Northern Colorado Writers, LLC

Cover photo by Scott Scofield
Cover design by Jennifer Top

Print ISBN: 978-0-578-64220-8
Ebook ISBN: 978-0-578-64222-2

To those who see the world through rhythm and rhyme–and the others who see reality as formless.

*~Imperfect humans
Can create a perfect world
Like so many trees~
(DKM)*

CONTENTS

Preface
The Pink Veil **1**
Poetry Seeks **2**
Ode To The Works In My Head **4**
Watermelon **7**
The Empty Pantry **8**
The Farm **12**
Over Easy **14**
A Writer's Fear **15**
Edge of Glory **17**
Twitter Poetry **20**
Sleeping in the Closet **21**
Symphony Concert **23**
In the… She does. **24**
Letter to Clouds on Fire **.25**
On the Way to Confession **27**
Current Affairs **29**
Wounded Soldiers **32**
Save the Sea **33**
Small Boys on Bikes **34**
Seven **36**
To Know Spring **37**

Lonely **38**
Strangers Lament **40**
Power Struggle **44**
Night Watch **46**
The Day After **47**
Winter visitors **49**
Don't Stare at Me **50**
Mother **52**
Edges of Words **53**
Words on Life **55**
Deep Woods **57**
Slipping Away **59**
How to Kiss Someone Without Revealing You Don't Like the Person You Are Kissing **60**
Wings **61**
Pine Needle Universe **63**
Haiku **64**
I Can Write With **65**
Catching the Mare **66**
Things I Carried **68**
Winter Wraith **69**
Gone Wild **71**
Buried Alive **72**
After **73**
Romance **74**
Irish Interlude **75**
Life is a Moving Train **77**
The Hill **80**
The Bus **81**
Tumble On **83**
Scribbled Rainbows **84**
A Small Life **85**
It's Different **87**
Once Majestic Spires **89**
Three A.M. **91**
The Pact **93**
Empty Fork **95**
The Miracle **97**
Treasures **98**

Clean **100**
The Move **101**
Active Shooter **102**
Apres Nam **104**
Heaven **107**
Middle School Art **108**
Dog Park **111**
Ancestors Take a Walk **113**
The Tracks We Leave Behind **116**
To Be **117**
Whispers of Nick **118**
A Triad of Ways **120**
There is Peace **121**
Contributor Biographies **123**
Acknowledgements **131**

PREFACE

The second edition of *Sunrise Summits* has been revised to fit the formatting and style of the Northern Colorado Writers anthology series. We have done our best to preserve the creative intent of the contributing poets and we apologize for any unintended and unavoidable changes to spacing and line breaks. Our hats off to all the poets who are represented in this book.

—Northern Colorado Writers

EDITOR'S COMMENTS

It is my distinct honor to assemble this anthology from the poets of Northern Colorado Writers (NCW). Now in its eleventh year, NCW continues to support writers of all genres and abilities in Northern Colorado and beyond. This first NCW poetry anthology exemplifies all that NCW strives to achieve. Included are works from award-winning poets, oft-published writers in other genres who are publishing their first poems, and poets whose work is being published for the first time.

Poetry is a fickle creature and the readers' interpretations even more so. I can neither speak for the writer, nor clarify their words for the reader. With this in mind, I have kept the editing to the bare minimum so that each poet's words are made available in their most pure form.

Given the wide variety of styles and topics selected for this anthology, my goal has been to present the poems in an order that gives each poem a chance to shine on these pages. I hope I have achieved this goal for both poem and poet.

Thank you for purchasing our first poetry anthology. Please let us know what you think via a posted review or other means.

Dean K Miller

Editor/Contributor

1

THE PINK VEIL

BY MONICA YOKNIS

Above the pure mantle of white
Drapes the gossamer veil of pink.
Blushing faces shine demurely through the haze.
The veil, is it falling or rising? I cannot say.
The light grows stronger, the pink veil brightens.
The mantle flashes with bright pink light.
The veil turns from pink to yellow.
Blushing faces disappear behind the now solid veil.
The sun has risen.
The mountains retreat behind their veil of blowing snow.

2

POETRY SEEKS

BY C. A. STRAZER

Poetry hears
Heart's silence.

Poetry stretches
Person's pose.

Poetry searches
Soul's caverns.

Poetry eases
Life's hurts.

Poetry sees
Hope's design.

Poetry awaits
Love's touch.

Poetry knows
Faith's promise.

Poetry seeks
Truth's glimmer.

Poetry defines
Life's purpose.

3

ODE TO THE WORKS IN MY HEAD
BY DINA BAIRD

Inspired in the moment, I write in my head.

So many works that appear and then float away.

Every day, I write so many things in my head, to capture them all would be madness.

So I set them free.

Some feel like sing-song poetry -

Lake, lake, river bottom, river bottom

Tree, know that your gift is appreciated even when the eagles have gone.

Many are questions that meander into personal essays -

Why does French Onion soup taste so good when the name sounds so gross? The first time I tried French Onion soup was today, at the age of 47, because French Onion soup sounds sour and briny and disgusting. I can't believe what I've been missing, but still, I know I'll need to be brave to taste the savory broth and cheese again.

Some of it is despair -

Relationships kill. This relationship is killing me.

Or perhaps it's my attitude that is killing me. Attitudes kill.

I am killing me.

Some of it is gratitude -

The green grass and melody of the birds

singing so politely and optimistic in the cool of morning.

The soft white floating fluffs featured by the sun as they float.

I don't even care about the yellow weeds and sneezes that come with their journey.

Turning my evening walk into a run just to watch the back of my daughter's hair flying in the wind,

the pink tassels on her white handlebars mark our summer celebration as I run behind her.

Piling turkey on wheat with pale tomatoes day-after-day to hear my son's "thanks mom."

Giving ride-after-ride to hear him laugh and talk with his friends about staying up late and how they don't ever get tired only to have them all fall asleep on the couch downstairs seconds later.

I know that time is wicked and soon enough they will be somewhere else and I'll only have these memories to keep me company.

These times are good. Today I am so thankful for this summer day.

Inspired in the moment, I write constantly in my head.

Words float like the white wisps of summer cotton and dandelion parachutes.

I'd miss so many things, unable to live in the present moment if I stopped to write them all down.

To the works that are never captured,

freedom for freedom.

4

WATERMELON

BY LORRIE WOLFE

Never wear a white blouse to a picnic. You'll get dirty.
~ Florence Berman

My grandmother stands
a gnarled goddess in her umbrella temple
bestowing fried chicken
like golden prizes to glowing champions

Their burnished cheeks
grin back in grateful tribute
as sun-drenched bodies plant themselves
on her flowered quilts

She slices home-made rhubarb pie
laughs, shrugs off the *hmmm* and *oh* of pleasured mouths
wrapping themselves in the bounty
her rolling pin has wrested
from earth, old oven, and encroaching arthritis

On that hot summer afternoon
I let the watermelon juice drip
from my bottom lip
and run inside the neck of my white cotton blouse

thinking about you

THE EMPTY PANTRY
BY S. E. REICHERT

I was raised in the shadow of a matriarch so strong and amazing
    I felt it only right to model myself on her salt-of-the-earth clay.
        To pride myself on practicing her never-ending attending.

But she died young.
    Younger than she should have.
        Her well ran dry.

Her pantry was empty.

It's no wonder she lost her mind,
    Rousing in the middle of the night to take out the silverware
        And sort it into plastic cups on the kitchen table.

Kicking off her socks in the cold asylum of the nursing home
    And laughing at the childlike memories looped around
        The empty spindle of her brain.

I used to want to be like her.
    A partner, an uncomplaining worker.
        A person who did what was necessary. Who barely sat down at meals
            For all the plate and need filling she did.

Such a tiny bird of a woman,
    Strong, vein-laced hands that could pull calves or mend fences.
    Nothing but leathered skin stretched over 206 bones.

But what did she want,
    In that space between bones?

No one ever knew.
    She died, an empty pantry,
        The secret still locked away, hiding on barren shelves.

Is that the better life?
    To die empty?
        To give all you have to those in need,
            Even when need turns to expectation?

To throw your body, your talents, your dreams, into the chaos,
    Let it swallow you in micro and massive bites at a time?

Now I feel her parched emptiness inside of my chest,
    Fingers run along dust-covered mantles.
        Breath blown into the cobwebs threaded across
        those sagging shelves,
            Residing in my heart.

Overdrawn my account and bankrupt my soul.
    Given so much, to so many, for so long that now they expect nothing less.
        And now, I have nothing more to give.

But the chaos cares not and it eats at me in new and faster swarms.
    Violent super storms, swirling into ever tightening
    masses
        Lightning stricken and burnt ground left beneath
        the rubble.

I don't know how to stop spinning,
    I don't know how to account, how to gather, how to replenish.
        I only know how to twirl, useless, in the hurricane's arms.

Letting it strip away at me inch and mile at a time.

    I shall leave nothing behind but an empty pantry.

6

THE FARM

BY KERRIE FLANAGAN

Grandma cooking, Grandpa plowing
Kids
Playing together
Gathering eggs, milking cows, feeding chickens

Grandma cooking, Grandpa plowing
Kids
Playing with friends
Gathering eggs, milking cows, feeding chickens

Grandma cooking, Grandpa plowing
Teens
Dating
Working in town, gathering eggs, milking cows, feeding chickens

Grandma cooking, Grandpa plowing
Young Adults
Moving away
Getting married, one left gathering eggs, milking cows, feeding chickens

Grandma cooking, Grandpa plowing
Adults
All moved away
No more chickens
No more cows

Grandma cooking, Grandpa plowing

Grandpa plowing

Empty farm

7

OVER EASY
BY KRISTI JOY

Eggs over easy with toast on the side.
Too much inside to speak of clearly
I'm not showing it.
Sipping hot beverages
Lips wet with speech
Toast crumbling
The morning paper too loud at my side
Feet jostling under my chair
Fork lifting eggs to my unspoken lips.

A WRITER'S FEAR
BY LORRIE WOLFE

After I disclose
all I can extract
from my own history
and dissect my original family

will my friends be
afraid to talk to me
lest they turn up
in my next story
twisted
but recognizable

What if Jen's sexy red dress
makes its entrance
obscenely stretched
over the bulging stomach of some
agéd beauty queen

and Inge's edgy laugh
explodes
from the mouth of a
black-leathered dominatrix
who holds the hero
bound hand and foot
while the real enemy absconds
with the antiquities.

Don't they know writing
is a lonely occupation?
When I am not with them
I conjure my friends around me
in a magic circle, while
there on the white page
my pen sings them
the only love song I know.

EDGE OF GLORY
BY KATHRYN MATTINGLY

They say God
doesn't give
you more suffering
than you
can bear.

I have seen
the suffering
some are given.
It only
makes this concept
more terrifying.

But then,
I have been
on that precipice
of mental anguish
to a point
where I could bear
no more
…and yet I did.

I only pray
the good Lord
does not
match in physical
pain
what I've
endured mentally
before I pass
through Heaven's
gate.

Life, of course,
isn't all suffering.
I would like to believe
everyone
who has suffered
mightily
has also visited
the edge of glory
at least once.

Life is
a balancing act.
Those who've seen
glory's edge
are also those
who swing low
into the depths
of despair.

But I'd rather
play boldly
from high to low
note, than live
my entire life
in the mid-range
of the scale.

Stuck in
Chopsticks,
afraid to
venture out
and rub coattails
with Chopin
… or Beethoven.

TWITTER POETRY
BY SHELLEY WIDHALM

140 characters to capture
My soul in a few words, a ballet dancer with a toehold to whirl, lines spinning out.
Send.

SLEEPING IN THE CLOSET

BY DR. NANCY REED

I have a friend
Who sleeps in a closet.
I don't know why,
But here's what I posit.

He leases the space
To save on rent,
'Cause by end of month
His paycheck's spent.

Maybe he likes
To feel comfy and cozy.
For him a tight space
Is homey and rosy.

Perhaps he feels safe
Being close to the walls.
Doesn't like immense rooms
Off long, drafty halls.

Maybe because
It's space he can manage,
Can adorn as he likes,
Which is an advantage.

He can dress up his closet
In the wink of an eye,
Sculpt with his socks,
Stack his shoes wide or high.

Hang colorful shirts
As his headboard of choosing.
The patterns of fabrics
Can be quite amusing.

Change the lighting by
Capping the bulb with a glove.
Dangle ties all around it
Make a mobile above.

Sometimes, I think,
It would be rather funny,
If he put in a skylight
So his closet is sunny.

I'm sure he's content
To live as he does,
Even though others
Create such a buzz.

Some think he's crazy,
But I think he's swell.
I don't worry about it.
He's happy and well.

SYMPHONY CONCERT
BY KERRIE FLANAGAN

The
notes
begin,
filling
the room,
slowly drifting up,
encircling overhead
covering us like a warm quilt
engaging our thoughts, memories, dreams
allowing us to be content if
only for a brief moment,
savoring the last
notes
as they
fade

slowly

away

IN THE... SHE DOES.
BY ZACHARY GILBERT

In the darkness of my dreams, she visits.
In the night where secrets bleed, she speaks.
In my hands I hide my crying eyes, she stares.
In my past, I had her killed, she forgives.

In the ocean of my minds sorrow, she swims.
In my dark soul she leaves her bright shadow.
In my grey hair like simmering smoke she runs her fingers.
In my ear she whispers, "Daddy don't cry, I love you."

LETTER TO CLOUDS ON FIRE
BY LAURA MAHAL

I've gotten out
of the place
of anger, as you advised.
Remembering to pray.
To be thankful for my blessings.
My husband, children,
home. But logic wasn't sufficient
to take me to new terrain.

I had to construct it.

I've inhabited my backyard, these many hours.
Carefully pruning away
dried stalks.
Seeking flashes of red, ladybugs rewarding me
for looking closely at what is always here.
The shovel a magnetic metal that insisted
I dig – uproot.
The flagstones didn't want to budge.

I grunted and heaved, casting out
cancer cells,
unkind words, ungenerous people.
Tilled diligently, combing
with my fingers to save
each earthworm I happened upon.
Segmented, these tunnelers, and I, too,
tunneled. Deeper into self.

Rebuilding the flagstone path
like a challenging 1,000-piece puzzle.
Seeking the shape that belongs,
then its sister, brother, cousin.
Setting aside that which does not,
as yet, align.
My heart pain lessens as my physical burdens
increase. Strain, flow, conscious intent
lean against the wall alongside a garden rake
and discarded gloves, holes in the fingertips.

ON THE WAY TO CONFESSION
BY JACQUELIN CORLISS

At the Buns on Wheels Food Truck, I wait for my burger.
The cook leans over the grill, reveals the space between his buttocks
and I feel ashamed, for looking, for saying I am a vegetarian.

Above, seagulls like tiny little brides—
one minute their wings fluttering behind as veils; the next,
a gray smudge surrendering to the swoon of
the impenetrable plumes of smoke rising
from the truck like a dream.

It's natural to be a carnivore, my friends say.

A man wears tweed pants and black rimmed glasses,
waits in line and watches me reach
for my burger on a wheat bun as thick as a pin cushion.
I'm reminded of the nuns who measured
our transgressions with the backside of a ruler,
blood purpling our palms.
Yes Sister, I am sorry Sister,
promising, promising.

I lift the burger to my mouth
grease flowering across the thin white plate.

Forgive me Father, for I have sinned.

16

CURRENT AFFAIRS

BY BELLE SCHMIDT

Always something to write about—
Apples, apparitions, apocalypse

Be it profound or simple.
Business letters are boring, boring, boring

Computers are parked on every desk,
Cursive writing has disappeared like the dodo bird.

Dare we even mention pride in penmanship?
Dictation to a secretary is seen only in old movies.

E-mail has changed the way we do business.
Efficiency is up with computers: debatable?

Filing was a basic skill taught in school, now go
Figure virtual folders, tool bars and iCloud

God help us!
Go back to school to learn word processing,

Hope for a passing grade
Hope I can remember all the jargon.

iPhone, who doesn't own one?
I've got information technology overload.

Just mastered Windows8, then it's updated
Joke's on me!

Keep smiling, I say to myself, and
Key in the memoir you've started.

Letter writing is something done in novels
Let's reminisce about love notes and diaries.

My autograph book is from 1956,
Mainly trite rhyming verses and well wishes.

Not very poetic and rather juvenile
Now these little tomes are extinct.

Oh, dear—maybe it's for the better.
Once life was simple, I miss those days.

Pope Francis has a twitter account,
Pray tell me what does it all mean?

Quirky is what I think.
Questions arise regarding hackers

Really scary listening to the news
Reports of government breaches,

Spies from North Korea and China
Servers and power grids are vulnerable

Time to explore emigrating to Mars
Take off in a rocket-propelled spaceship

Ultimate destruction of planet Earth, due to
Underutilized brain power and no common sense.

Victory is the survival of the species
Valiant, fearless, courageous to the end.

We colonize Mars and other planets
We humans are **not** replaced by robots.

Xanadu in outer space is our new home,
"X" marks it on celestial maps.

Yes, our trajectory is somewhere out there for
You and me and our children and grandchildren.

Zero hour, as predicted and depicted, does arrive.
Zany ending.

WOUNDED SOLDIERS
BY C. A. STRAZER

Wounded soldiers torn apart
By the war, you didn't start
Come to Healing Waters
All you sons and daughters
Hurt by vileness we didn't see
Join us today for a day to be
Blessed by Heaven above
Fishermen filled with love
Patiently teaching their art
Fly fishing they'll impart
Pain soon turns to joy
When a soldier employs
A cast too good to ignore
And a fish begins to soar
Through air to waiting net
The wounded soldier to get
And forget for now his sad regret
Pain, terror his sorrowful debt.

SAVE THE SEA
BY SUMMER ROBIDOUX

Bobbing on the water's surface, peaceful and serene,
Birds flutter above, enjoying the breeze.
Atop, little white crests show the ocean's drive;
It's active, dynamic, and absolutely alive.
Scales glimmer and sparkle as a fish jets through.
Constantly keeping an ever-watching eye,
Looking for foes in both the water and the sky.
In the distance a sea turtle trudges along.
Appearances deceiving, looking strong and well,
The animal, it turns out, is pasty and pale.
With a belly full of plastic bits and pieces,
The food he ate an hour ago goes undigested.
Starving to death, the creature searches,
Nutrition unobtainable makes the reptile despondent.
Soon he will still and not a thought will be shared,
Of the animal that was killed
As the human above tosses another plastic container
While shopping, milling unaware.
So please reduce, reuse, and recycle with care,
And smile contently as you think of the sea life that will be spared.

SMALL BOYS ON BIKES
BY PATRICIA WALKER

This evening the clouds were heavy grey pillows
pregnant with more of the afternoon's thundershowers waiting
to release their tempers once again
on summer sidewalks still sporting an occasional puddle
like a black eye after a fight.

And as I walked along, two boys about eight or ten
zigged past me displaying their little-boy bicycle skills
(no doubt for my benefit)
leaving tiny trails like alligator tails
from the treads of their tires. The skinny one's
Rockies cap obscured his hair

obscured his care
that this middle-aged woman walking
might once have had a boy or two just like him,
a boy who used to wait for the school bus on the corner,
come home for dinner every evening,

a boy she used to haul to baseball practice and soccer games,
a boy who, with a sheepish grin and a dirty face
would bring her bouquets of yellow dandelions which she'd proudly
display in a cup full of water
on the kitchen table.

SEVEN

BY DORIS MILLER

A little tyke for his age
Standing below the baptismal font
Straining to see what's inside
Not hearing his new father's words
Of new baptismal life
Reaching up and grabbing the bowl
Pedestal tipping
Water splashing Darrell's shirt
Is there enough water left
For baptism on his forehead?
Maybe if there had been enough water
He wouldn't be drowning in alcohol now
Fifty-five

TO KNOW SPRING

BY LORRIE WOLFE

To know spring
first know winter

Wake the pine
Know this place

Snowflakes and tulips
pas de deux

Winter
loses again

22

LONELY

BY JUNE CAROLUS

lonely can
pull from reality
a position
of dreams that won't come true
wither
in complete exhaustion
bring
stand still-alone
take away
passion to live
proficiently removes
catalogs of pages
time is
only numbers on a clock
categories sliced
in a decoupage of stillness
without
an ear to listen
lonely chases Alone
to a dead end
tears
the epitome of lost

sorrow
from within drains
engages
one on one
lonely seeps
into crevices of a soul
leaving it
open to feel deserted
a spirit astray
in solitary
lonely attacks

23

STRANGERS LAMENT

BY KATHRYN MATTINGLY

Oh to unlock the heart and open the mind of a potential friend. Granted, a stranger momentarily. Because, well, the person in question is new …new to town, new to the 'group.' It's a new life and new adventure for lucky YOU! Dare to dream they care about your *feelings* while basking in the fine glow of forever friends who are hovering here and there at the 'meeting' where you are simply the 'newbie.'

How do I communicate the
hard truths and my uneasy
thoughts? What can make
meaningful conversations
happen? What will free my
spirit and cause my suddenly
encumbered soul to soar
among those who are too
terribly comfortable in their
zone to zoom in and focus
on a lost-looking creature,
dismembered from recently
being uprooted, if they even
remember from where or why.

I am sad to have already
burned bridges, yet glad to
have spoken what was on
my mind, although it was
not comprehended in a
caring way. I hate it when
the obvious becomes clear.
I despise that some would
make no effort to understand
or somehow iterate the
irritating difficulties of
being 'new.' Why can't we
rise above our 'selfness' and
interject empathy into the mix?

When will a few brave others
forge a pathway to those inner
thoughts of a new face? Use
the golden opportunity to
merge a small moment of
our momentous individual
journeys? Why do we hide
within our inhibitions instead
of bravely being a beacon
to someone in search of light,
any light to warm an icy chill
felt by the singled-out stranger?
If only we'd walk a minute
in someone else's hours.

Then perhaps we'd understand
how stepping over ourselves
to stop a stranger from
stumbling in the dark night
of a recently reconstructed
reality might make all the
difference. If only just one
someone would try and
fill the empty always aching
wish for a caring person
to sip coffee with, and share
the niceties of normal.
Dare I say it might lead to
volumes of mutual venting?

This is what bonds us, blocks
built from comparing trivia, true
confessions and shared time.
Not a big thing, sharing time,
but a valued thing when you
have no one to share your
precious time *with*, no one but
that one or some ones who will
take the time to form a new
friendship, bravely cross the
lonely stranger line with a
warm smile (I daresay) more
needed than the necessary latte
used to create the muse.

POWER STRUGGLE

BY NANCY L. REED

You shove.
I stand firm.
You push.
I must yield.

You bear down.
I bend further.
You drive harder.
I refuse to break.

I twist into a distortion of myself
And do not like what I am becoming.
I will not transform to suit you,
Refuse to change to what you want me to be.

I respond in kind,
Determined to resist you.
I am alarmed by my intent
To overpower you.

I could force you
But can't accept breaking you.
I will not push that far.
There is only one choice.

I welcome serenity's possession.
Your desire to dominate is powerless.
Our connection is broken
And will never exist again.

NIGHT WATCH
BY ELEANORE TRUPKIEWICZ

Strength in a thimble
what a mouse carries
when he slips away

Dead of night
and all I could see
your ghost in the hall

Cricket song rippling
along unpainted walls
and scarred baseboards

Moonlight lay tracks
across the place where
your pillow should be

and now is not
will never be

and for all my sins
I blame you.

THE DAY AFTER
BY KARI REDMOND

I
This is not the end, he said
She knew it too

The essence alone
Brought her back

Was it feeling or fancy?
Difficult to tell
Either indulged by so few.

They always tried not to call it
Their own.

II
Their age is not important
It rarely ever is.
One walks with a cane,
The other does not.

He wandered through a field of lilies
Hopeful the scent alone would bring it back.

Until, like a whim
It reached her
On wings he hadn't yet imagined

The direction of his voice
Confused her.

It wasn't lilies, it was mangos

WINTER VISITORS
BY SHELLEY WIDHALM

When the blackbirds stayed,
tail feathers inked the white page
of Nebraska's plains.

DON'T STARE AT ME
BY KERRIE FLANAGAN

You know who I am…

I am the girl with no hair on my head
I am the boy who has a wheelchair for legs
I am the daughter who speaks with my hands
I am the son who needs crutches to stand.

On the outside I do look different
But on the inside I am the same.
I laugh
I cry
I feel joy.
And pain

I want to be noticed
For the great things I do.
For the nice person I am
And for my talents too.

Next time you see me
Please don't stare
Just send me a smile
Show me you care.

MOTHER

BY ZACHARY GILBERT

Icy water, cold and fast, moves over smooth rocks,
Its wet bite engulfs my bare feet.
Falling to my knees I beg, "River, weep with me!"
My hand warms as it blocks the yellow glow.
My eyes ache; I scream fatigued words, "Sun!
Where is your murky black veil of cloud?"
I climb over dusty sharp rocks,
Broken wood cuts hot blood from my cheek.
My pain is all around, in anger I whisper,
"Mountains, hollow out. Empty yourself, be like my soul.
Earth, why do you not burst? Can't you feel the agony all around me?
You take no notice."
Pine Trees dance in the wind, the silence of existence.
My Mother's agony, in her end, saturates my invisible pain.

EDGES OF WORDS
BY KARI REDMOND

On the edges of words
You spoke so softly
I have trouble remembering
The truth within them

Where what is not said
Means more
Where words float to fill the space between
You and me
Where forever once belonged

On the edges of boundaries we were always testing
Pushing like a rubber band
You from me
Me from you
The edges became blurred
Like the crayon drawing your niece gave me
Outside the lines, we were magic

On the edges of love as we defined it
On the border between your heart and your head
Where moments became memories
Piled into years
I thought there'd be time for always

There on the edge of the bed, what used to be ours
sometimes, only sometimes
I hear the words you tried to say
The whisper on the edges you kept to love me
And I forgive you

WORDS ON LIFE

BY DEAN K MILLER

Lifeless print
Sparks suspicions
Humbles heroes
Dictates despair
Evokes emotions
  Sad
    Happy
      Angry
        Hopeful
          Insecure
            Confident
              Jealous
                Love

Life–
Hinges on words
Describing scenery
Expressing opinions
Giving direction
Communicating emotions
  Outbursts
    Apologies
      Insults
        Compliments
          Limitations
            Encouragement
            Hate
              Love
Life–
Expired, breathless
Stale, unmoving
Nothing left
To say but
Unconscious words
  Dead
    Lifeless
      Words
        That
          Do
            Not
              Express
              Love.

DEEP WOODS
BY PATRICIA WALKER

You sound just like my relative, the one
with the Midwest hair.
The accent comes from tramping through thorny, waist-high bushes,
drinking beer with tin labels,
skinning pungent kills with "the guys."

You slide your tongue and your mind into my mouth
but I don't bite.
I have learned to tune your guitar by ear,
bend your canoe waiting for you to tether it
at the branch,
crank your rock music under pierced eyebrows.

I never knew you had it in you.
It comes from locomotives blowing
through the back yard all night;
no one notices the tracks in the snow beyond the kitchen window.
The lights are on inside and they all chat smoking,
except me.

Please don't teach it to the children.
Oh hell, they've already heard it, packed
in with the marshmallows.
The smell of green canvas harmonizes with the song of the loon
varnishing the lake.

SLIPPING AWAY
BY KRISTI JOY

White snow
melting
dripping
pooling into pockets
of unmet heartbreak.

Distance
looming
crouching
pouncing on
my open, bleeding heart.

Rain keeps falling
as steam rises
from this soft melting snow.
I try to keep it there
grasping, pushing
willing it to stay
as I helplessly watch it
slip away.

HOW TO KISS SOMEONE WITHOUT REVEALING YOU DON'T LIKE THE PERSON YOU ARE KISSING

BY JACQUELINE CORLISS

I once opened the freezer and wrote your name in the snow.
You said I was an exclamation mark, last,
in a long line of vowels and consonants.

Tell myself—
nothing left now but your book beside the bed.
A page in the last chapter folded over.

I remember. Your words in my ear.
Felt like thin blades of grass pushing
through concrete.
You, as proud as a high-back leather chair,
my fingers splayed across your chest.
I lean in, let you pull the back of my hair.
Open my mouth and paint your tongue gold.
This is what it feels like.
Snowflakes on a frying pan.

WINGS

BY SHELLEY WIDHALM

I rip pages out
of my notebook
and close it.

Hummingbirds
        stationary
in their feeding
go nowhere.

What is my question
before I breathe in
the sunset splattered with almost
anything.
Wings go all blurry
as the decision of which
flower to pick
makes me go still
until I ask what if.

The song
Free to Decide
lets me loose on the edge of their wings
on the lift
until I turn to the next blank page.

It's then I find my flight
in the choices and lines
and where to
let the song

Fly.

PINE NEEDLE UNIVERSE
BY S. E. REICHERT

The wind through pines reverberates the sea,
Its quickening wildness like waves to the shore.
An entirety of an ocean in a single tree

Echoing in soft rushes above me as blood in veins
Or mother's heart beat in womb.
Timeless recognition of the universe rippling through us both.

Ancient before and beyond me
It speaks to the silent soul
Who's battled long enough

We forget the peace within us,
Until we stop to listen
And hear it whispering outside us.

HAIKU
BY BEN HUMPREY

One hears
the Tao in a silent
onomatopoeia

I CAN WRITE WITH

BY SHEALA DAWN HENKE

I can write with
A turntable of hope
The means to an end,
Some fault lines of change
An adaptation of reality,
A cross country path
A firing squad of synapses,
Brittle tidbits of imagination
To bring them to their knees.

CATCHING THE MARE
BY PAM WOLF

I hold the old halter
early quiet …drifting along
step soft slow
seek the grazing white mare
through early morning fog
not to startle her
my boots lift
hover just above the ground

My thoughts move back
black earth
dry grass
the pasture
I try to see how
it once was
I nod my pleasure
to the earth… I thank
the winter sun
the wind's hint of warmth
the shortened darkness

elusive fox, gray coyotes,
mustangs, Bison of long ago
left their tracks in this earth
along with the grasses
only a few, like the mare
remain

even some like me leave my footprints
and still can't comprehend the gift

pasture musing

THINGS I CARRIED
BY ELEANORE TRUPKIEWICZ

a wheel of bruised
dreams

the same nightmare
on a loop

your lies like
a leaden weight

scars in a cascaded
constellation

the stillness a ghost
has, and has not
is and is not

a barrel of blame
an ocean of ashes.

WINTER WRAITH

BY S. E. REICHERT

I am only a smattering of bones.
A carcass stretched tight in leather clothes.
A rattling memory
Of vibrant youth
Of the hopeful waves of spring

Now sits in winter and watches a bitter December
Through frost coated and blue iris windows.

I am a lesion too long festered
Now rotted and won
Over a once easy soul

I am laid waste along a barren horizon
Old pointy shards digging
Into the earth, pitting the crust of leaf and pine needle beds.
        Pausing in brittle repose, before death fully claims her.

How did I go so this way?
How was it I never turned back on this road?
Never questioned the twisting inked path, leading me into such inescapable wilderness?
        How desolate, a life misjudged.

A creeping swarm breaks from the delicate cage of my ribs,
Bursting out,
        The last passionate exhale left me.

So sad that it should happen in the darkness, alone.

GONE WILD

BY SHEALA DAWN HENKE

In my wildest dreams
It gnashes its teeth at any
Barrier.
To rip through layers of the dull,
Boring, dry wall
Of No Words.

BURIED ALIVE
BY KRISTI JOY

The bones have yellowed and cracked
taking up the slack on the inside.
Old and betrayed
withered and decayed
knowing their place
in the thick of it.

Too lost to see
what the truth is.

Juicy flesh dripping
clawing and ripping
to escape
not knowing what the point is.

While buried and quiet
dirt resting and cool
the heart pumps
its hot blood
to my mouth.

AFTER

BY ZACHARY GILBERT

The intensity of him washes tension out of my body,
As I lead him into the secret valley, my soft soul exposed.
Reality dissolves, stress dies, its funeral foggy,
Linens in chaos, my soul's peace composed.

His voice deep and smooth, like a waterfalls thunder,
Goose bumps dance all over my neck and arms.
His eyes soft, his soul lifted, and I see under.
Secrets saturate the night, I soak in his charms.

Love becomes; heat, breath, and silence,
Moments mortality fades, amid my defiance.

ROMANCE

BY ELEANORE TRUPKIEWICZ

Expect starless nights
squalls in our ocean
no lighthouse on shore
in the seamy darkness.

Expect rainfall and
blizzarding snow on
the day we first part
and every day after.

Expect sunshine not
at all because this world
does not promise us
the sun or the moon.

Expect rainbows only
when we have lasted
to the end of the night,
endured until morning.

IRISH INTERLUDE
BY PAMELA WOLF

Connnemera Coast, Ireland

we race along a slender slice
of wild Irish beach.
I ride easy, sit lightly
on the broad back of a
spirited Gypsy horse

we gallop steady
hoof prints mark wet sand.
tangled thick mane teases my face
we lean into the wind.

Unruly clouds, sidestep
away from us, shift,
toss bits of sunlight, shadow
over layers of emerald hills

spread out on the horizon
like a patchwork quilt
thrown casually
over rising slopes.

they blur quickly by,
noisy gulls chase
surf that surges
recedes only to return
unleashed, wearing wings.

breath pulses
in ... and out of us, like the sea
blood courses through our veins
unused to such passion.

Ireland

LIFE IS A MOVING TRAIN
BY KATHRYN MATTINGLY

Life is a moving train
- a continual
sensation.
And you and me,
we stopped together
at every station.

Our first
layover
- the Oregon
Coast, with its
misty shorelines
and lighthouse
ghosts.

Then the rain-soaked
Willamette Valley
where our babies
grew up to be
train station savvy,
riding rails of
their own.

We packed our bags
for prickly days
of painful priorities
in the complex
maze of pristine
Portland, until
I bailed.

My lone stop
was East of Eden,
where grapes of
plenty soothed
my wrath and
wrapped me in
fragrant goodness.

You came
on a different train
down the road a ways
and saved us. We
savored a few
sun-soaked years
until jobs dried up.

The train strained
to a new normal.
It wound back
to Oregon.
Snow-covered peaks
pierced our hearts,
renewed our resolve.

We prayed to
let the train stay
wedged in
the quiet cracks.
But the whistle
wailed and we
were gone again.

Life is a moving
train until the last
bend in the track,
when the conductor
calls you back
home again
at journey's end.

But I will write
upon the wind
that if I could,
I'd buy a ticket
for the same
train. Yes,
I would.

And with you
by my side
my lover,
my friend
I'd climb aboard
and…
I'd ride it again.

THE HILL

BY SUMMER ROBIDOX

Trekking along, pursuing your dreams
Minutes become days, which mold into years.
Soon the metaphoric hill that everyone dreads
Is close in proximity and you've nowhere to veer.
Reaching the summit and gazing about
Surprisingly, the view is lively and bright,
And suddenly life's priorities are crystal clear:
Faith and family, friends and the Earth hold dear.
The house, the car, the job is now slight.
When did their significances lose its might?
Creating relationships is what makes us rich;
Dump the stuff, the excess, and the façade,
And live a life of service, gratitude and love.
Invest in our children, animals, and land

Giving the future the most you can.

THE BUS

BY JENNIFER J. GOBLE, PH.D.

The hum of the motor
The silence in the air
The stopping
The starting
The jerking
The Bus
The people get on
One by one
Some pay with money
Some with a pass
Some get a pass back
Some say good morning
Most are silent
Silent they sit
They think
They sleep
They wait
I wonder what they think
I wonder where they go
Some bring coffee
Some bring food
Some have backpacks

One has a red hat
One looks familiar
All are silent
The sound
The light
The stop
They get off
One gets off at the hospital
One at Monico
Many get off at high school
One at junior high
Two at community college
And me…
I pull the cord
The sound
The light
I gather my books
My coffee
The doors open
I arrive

TUMBLE ON

BY MONICA YOKNIS

Ah, the tumbleweed!
Rolling, bouncing, dipping and dodging.
Where the wind blows, so the tumbleweed.
The poignant, iconic tumbleweed,
Where would the American West be without you?
Crosser of highways,
Clogger of fences,
Our beloved,
Perfect (if prickly),
Ubiquitous tumbleweed.
Tumble on, tumbleweed

SCRIBBLED RAINBOWS
BY JUNE CAROLUS

an empty page evolves
as I pick up the crayons
to fill in my coloring book
crayons and paper clash
blue, green, purple and pink
wrap around each other
completing a quartet
colors fade into each other
as the turning of a page
unfolds an image of little hands
tracing invisible pictures
glides across the paper
like a paint brush connects dot to dot
drawing outside the lines
a masterpiece of scribbled rainbows
blend a signature of creation

A SMALL LIFE

BY PAM WOLF

pale dry leaves cushion a spot
under the butterfly bush
a leafy cave
hides a dark place…

from my kitchen window
I see a slight gray shadow
tall ears above a pink nose
I'm startled as two eyes
stare at me from under the bush

a rabbit… frozen as a statue
not blinking
safe in its stillness
in perfect camouflage hawks won't
see as they fly overhead
looking for dinner
I say hello and in an instant
it hops away
into the grass and weeds beyond
as if it heard me speak

evening flows in, moves the day
out of the way
I sense something watching
prepare supper and glance out the window
there it is again
stares through the window
curious I suppose
I smile and move

to see if it will turn its head to follow
this time just a flicker of its eye
the rabbit has claimed this spot
I see its small gray form every morning
and evening for days
sometimes it spends the day there
happily nibbling on seeds and grass
crabapples spread over the ground
never moving far from its hiding place

In the middle of the night
I hear an animal scream.
it isn't a dream
nor the first time I hear this sound
filter through my sleep

when you live near farms and fields
out beyond the lights and noises of the city
the sharp sadness of loss
the beat of life and death is always present
in small ways

IT'S DIFFERENT

BY LAURA MAHAL

Where I come from – it's different.
There's no soccer.
Just drive-by shootings.
After four in the afternoon, kids keep their heads down.
Below window level. Two kids
died when I was in fifth grade.
They was sitting at the table, doing homework.
Then they was nothing but blood on the floor.
No more.

Where I come from, I didn't take no Home Ec.
There were no teacher's pets or 3-D printers.
But I could upper cut, and cross. Feint, and jab.
I lost three teeth when I was a sophomore.
That's all that boyfriend took from me.
He knocked up an eighth-grader. She gave him her trust, and he gave
her a baby girl.
That's all he gave her for her fourteenth birthday.
A pink rattle and some food stamps.

I pay $500 bucks for my son to play soccer.
Plus, he needs cleats and a uniform and to be driven to some other city every weekend.

My daughter, she take Karate. That costs $100 a month.
The uniform was free.
But she don't need it in no 0-9 month size, and she wear a mouth guard. The most she ever got was a busted lip.

My son, he ain't got a gun and he's never spent the night in the county jail for shoplifting.
He just go to his friends' houses for playdates.
I got me a nice smile these days, implants and all. My teeth are snow-white and so is my life.

My kids ask me, "Mama, didn't you ever play soccer?"
I just say,
"It was different."

ONCE MAJESTIC SPIRES
BY DORIS MILLER

Once majestic spires of emerald green
Now standing ugly brown,
    Dead upright
    Upright dead
    Beetle-kill
Once handsome men of blue-green eyes
Now humped limp dishrags,
    Dead memory
    Dementia dead
    Parkinson- kill
People spraying the green pines
    Stop the beetles
    Boring in the bark
Planes spraying Iowa's green corn
    Stop the corn-borer
    Sneaking up the stalks
Brothers pumping DDT on mattresses
    Kill the crunchy bedbugs
    Creeping up the crevices

Ground water seeping DDT
    Tiristy people swallowing
    My brother, my sister-in-law,
    My husband
    Fingers trembling, feet stumbling
    Parkinson's
"Mom, I have to tell you something,
 Sit down and listen.
    I have Parkinson's."
    Age 49, Diane
Once a vibrant young lady
Now despairing tiredness,
    Hands shaking, legs quivering
    Parkinson's

THREE A.M

BY DEAN K MILLER

It's three a.m. and I'm naked.
This is only a concern
because I am not dreaming
and don't know where I am.

Except –

I stand before a small window
listen to the rain
ping off the metal roof.
Something seems familiar.
The weather? Or where I stand?

Searching for clues I find
I'm in a bathroom
that is too small to
afford any luxuries.

But –

The toilet is functional
which yields no other hints.
No, the answer to this mystery
lies outside. Two cars are parked
where there is usually only one.

That much I remember.
Wait until I tell the kids that.

The Kids –

That's right, one of them
is coming to visit. See! I do
Remember.
But why two cars
if only one is coming?
More answers mean more questions,
questions I cannot answer.

I hate this confusion – this
Mix-up of my life. Everything changes,
sometimes every day.
But no one else
seems to notice.

THE PACT

BY BELLE SCHMIDT

The Sun is strong in Death Valley. It scorches the Land and sucks every drop of moisture from its surface. It is a malevolent Sun intent on shriveling human beings leaving only their whitened skulls to mark their passage.

It is honoring a strange pact entered into with Earth—to annihilate Man, the species that are the Ultimate Great Destroyers. They wreak destruction on the Land. Man is the enemy. Sun and Earth aim to erase human beings from the face of Earth and to return them to dust.

Man's power lies in his machines. With this power, he topples mountains, flattens forests, dissolves islands, and parts the ocean with spears which sink deep. He kills Nature and covers Earth with a grey shell.

Birds will no longer nest in the Great Mother's hair, animals will no longer find shelter in her bosom and ocean denizens will no longer play in the waters at her feet.

Earth and Sun envision the Mother's death and believe
it to be inevitable. That is why they feel compelled to interfere.
They *must!*
The apathetic attitude of humans will lead to decimation and
extinction of all creatures. This dire prediction, if allowed
to be fulfilled, will be a painful pitiful end filled with suffering.
The Land will heave and writhe and roar in its agony.

Therefore, Sun and Earth have entered into an alliance which
highlights their common interest. Their sworn pact is to eliminate
these beings, called Man, who consistently and systematically
rape Mother Earth. They abuse her sacredness and exhibit a
lack of respect which is monumental. A sacrilege!
Sun and Earth avow to avenge these actions.

After Human Beings are gone, Sun and Wind will scourge the surface
of the Earth. Sun will turn on its centillion-wattage. Oceans
will evaporate, glaciers and icebergs will melt. Wind will sweep
away all vestiges of Man. Earth will become a blank canvass.

Creation can begin again.

EMPTY FORK

BY DORIS MILLER

His fork goes slowly toward his mouth
There's nothing on it
Four-five time he tries
Closes his mouth and swallows nothing.
The fork skims around the edge of the plate
Jabs the flowers but they don't move.
A dab of potato on the fork
Falls off on his apron
Over and over he tries to rescue
The spilled dab
Searching the patterned cloth.
I try to take his fork to help him
His grip tightens
And he says the one word
Spoken the entire meal,
"No."
I jab the steak with my fork
And bring it toward his lips
He open his mouth like a baby bird
Chews and swallow real food.
Over and over I bring my fork to his mouth

Feeding my baby bird.
My steak and potatoes are cold
I'm not hungry anymore
Maybe we'll have steak and eggs for breakfast.

THE MIRACLE

BY JENNIFER J. GOBLE, PH.D.

My first memory is the fear and excitement of the unknown.
Next is the question, "Is it time?" Every move is a chore.
Rushing, wondering, scared, happy, thinking, planning.
The emergency room, "Where is it?" "Go to the east of the building."
Hollow, white, sterile, skinny beds, heavy women, lots of chrome.
Gadgets everywhere. Oh the pain! Scared, panic, what the hell!
Soft touches, pats, smiles, buttons to push, a clock to watch.
Strangers come and go, check machines, speak to others
like I'm not there.
He paces, asks questions, looks worried, acts secure, watches T.V.
Oh the pain in my back. Nobody told me about the pain. Damn them.
18 hours of pain. I hate them for not telling me, warning me.
Rushing again. "It's time! Call him, call him! Hurry!
Don't! Breathe! Count! Don't! Breathe! Just breathe!
Push! Now you can push"
"Don't tell me what to do!"
Oh my God!

The joy!
The exhaustion!
The miracle!

TREASURES
BY PATRICIA WALKER

Jaime has a personal letter from his hero, Bobby Orr,
that cost too much money to have framed,
but he had to get the best acid-free paper and non-glare glass
to hold the display so it would last
one hundred years or more

My father has a cigar box full of military pins
and campaign buttons proclaiming, "I like Ike" before it was popular.
In his basement there are crates of antique car parts
such as lanterns and a horn that barks
"ay-oo-ga."

I have color photos and "Sammy Hagar"
scribbled in black marker on everything from ball caps
to guitar picks and spiral notebooks to the sky.
What will happen to them when I die?
I know the words by heart.

On the floor in the closet there are boxes
of my children's tiny faces and crayon dreams,
report cards and levels of learning how to swim.
My grandfather was a writer; have you ever heard of him?
Of course not.

Will my memories fall like a pebble into a stream
and settle to the bottom without a sound,
the ripples' cadence losing time as it moves towards the shore?
Is it naught for all, or
will they stir

up a sandy spot and keep on rolling
until they are washed into the sea,
a larger being than simply me?
Maybe that explains why I always have to get my feet wet.

CLEAN

BY JENNIFER GOBLE, PH.D.

It's the smell of a *baby* after her bath
prayer while you kneel alone
freshness of flowers
healing of words
symmetry of life as we've known

It's *acceptance* of loved ones
fallen new *rain*
shirts ironed with *starch*
smiles from strangers
new thoughts after the pain

It's the feeling of *pleasure* after the run
rest at the close of a day
sounds among *birds*
moments of *beauty* we treasure
sunshine where the land greets the rays

THE MOVE

BY SUMMER ROBIDOUX

My heart is breaking a little today,
For I just found out that my kids are moving away.
They must forge ahead and make their own path,
Fulfill their destiny and start giving back.
My brain can rationalize their choices,
But my heart protests their decision.
I don't care if you are grown!
I don't care if you can make it on your own!
I want you near to enjoy you my dears.
I pout and I plea, but they shake their heads adamantly;
It's of no use, clearly I can see.
As a last ditch effort I try to compromise:
Go if you must; I wish you nothing but the best,
But please, I beg, leave the grandkids with me!

ACTIVE SHOOTER
BY BELLE SCHMIDT

Bang. Pop. Pop. Shooter in the classroom
Bang. Pop. Pop. Shooter in the classroom
Students rush to hide in the library
Students rush to hide in the library
Pop. Pop. Students rush the shooter,
Rush in the classroom, to hide in library.

Lock the doors. Call 9-1-1. Help!
Lock the doors. Call 9-1-1. Help!
Sobs and tears. Fear is all around
Sobs and tears. Fear is all around
The doors lock. Call help. 9-1-1
All around is fear, tears and sobs

Riot police with bullet-proof vests arrive
Riot police with bullet-proof vests arrive
Ambulances remove dead and wounded
Ambulances remove dead and wounded
Bullet-proof ambulances. Police dead.
Remove vests. Wounded arrive.

Arrive in classroom and library. Pop. Pop
9-1-1 police rush around and help. Pop.
Remove dead shooter. Students
Wearing bullet-proof tears, bang, bang doors,
Lock and hide. All wounded fear. Sobs.

APRES NAM
BY NANCY L. REED

<u>Classroom Memory (September 1973)</u>

You weren't in class.
    No.
Are you alright?
    No.
May I ask where you were?
    No.
Will this happen again?
    Yes.
More than once?
    Yes.
Can you let me know beforehand?
    No.
Well, let's see how it goes.

    I'm sorry I wasn't in class.
Yes?
    I guess I'll have to drop out.
Really?
    I'll be gone again. I can't help it.
Why?

> *I need to tell you where I go.*
>
> Where?
>
> > *There is a room, safe and still. I go there when I remember.*
>
> Remember?
>
> > *The things that haunt me till I scream.*
>
> Scream?
>
> > *About what I saw and what I did.*
>
> [Silence]
>
> > *I throw myself against the padded walls to dull the memories.*
>
> [Silence]

I'm sorry this happened to you.
> *Yes.*

Is there anything I can do to help?
> *No.*

There must be something.
> *No.*

I can listen.
> *No.*

You won't speak of it again?
> *No.*

I'll be here.
> *Yes.*

Will you ever come back?
> *No.*

[Silence]
> *[Silence]*

Classroom Memory (November 1973)

He sits tensed, unmoving in the straight-back, metal chair outside the classroom door,
Staring from the hallway, through the room, out the window and beyond.
> Beyond the withered forsythia obscuring the smudged window,
> Beyond the asphalt lot of toxin-spewing vehicles,
> Beyond Old Main menacing the barren hilltop.

Beyond …

> … to the dripping jungle, buzzing with urgent,
> raspy-throated whispers
> … to the cluster of injured, hunched bodies and
> mounds of the dead
> … to his existence in that nightmarish horror
> movie, real and surreal.

His desolate profile compels us, pulls us toward him in the hallway.
In an effort to comfort him, we drive him to panic and must retreat.
He cannot come to us who are encased in walls.
We cannot go to him who becomes caged by our bodies.
We must retreat and leave him to his isolation.

> He served with honor in the jungle,
> Killing, running, hiding.
> He was changed forever.
> Bloody, broken bodies torment his memories.
> Anguished, desperate cries invade his sighs.

Impending Memories (Future Time)

The classroom is filled with children's shrill voices.
Three students huddle over a book.
The teacher told them to pick a book of fiction,
But the violence in this book excites and enthralls,
As much fiction to them as the fantasies they read.
At recess, they clash in mock battle.
At home, they skirmish in their electronic games
And hone their skills for long-distance battles,
Oblivious to the horrific damage of actual combat.

They share forbidden candy bars and smudge the pages of the book
On the history of war, photos included,
Speak excitedly about their graphic novels full of bombs and guns,
And brag about what they would do with such glorious weapons.

Can they distinguish people from pixels?

HEAVEN

BY KARI REDMOND

Denise had a place called heaven,
You could go there and it was like time wrapped itself in a bottle.
You could throw it overboard and watch it drift away.

I remember it the way you tell stories years later.
Facts are distorted to make way for the way you wish it had been.
Who remains to tell the truth?

I like to think maybe someday an old man might find that bottle,
fishing off the coast of Miami, it might catch his eye.

What I really remember most about heaven,
was never knowing what time it was.
Getting in the car and not believing the clock on the dash.
I wish most of my life were like this.

Maybe the fisherman will open it up, sit in the sand
And call it heaven.

MIDDLE SCHOOL ART
BY RENATE HANCOCK

She hangs on the wall by my desk,
sculpted of aluminum wire.
Curls of copper shavings slant across
heart-shaped torso,
stretched into fragile breastplate.
Disdained project of middle school,
nibbled at the heart by transient friends who leave
shreds behind like mice nests hidden
in corners parents never see.

A single vein circulates
to feet spread wide
struggling to find balance
as wave after wave of labels and ridicule
strip her flesh in anorexic cravings,
dislodging her faith in the beauty
and mystery of her form.

Copper wool winds around
the crown of her head, a halo of ginger
above a face invisible,
blending into the wall behind her.
Every moment hoping to escape notice
every moment unnoticed
becoming more indistinct.

Her arms stretch wide, like a paper doll—
no longer linked
to childhood companions.
From a distance, she reflects
the shape of a five pointed star;
look closer, and see
empty arms

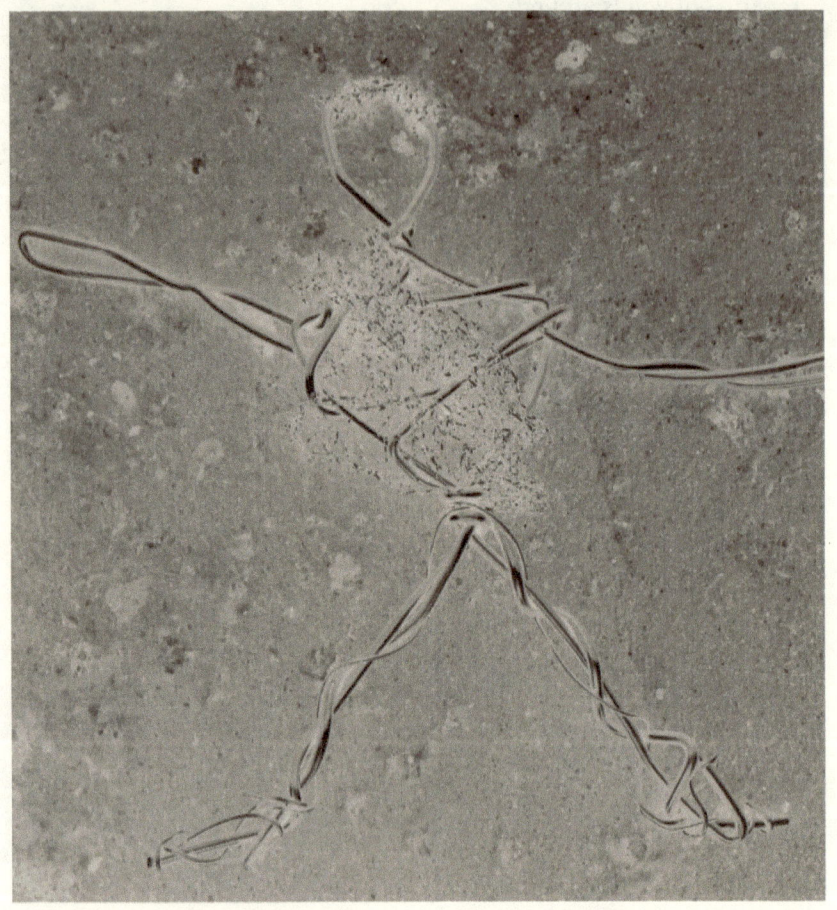

DOG PARK

BY BEN HUMPHREY

In Dickensonian light,
she opens the gate,
enters without leash
or collar.

Stands in the back,
eyes follow the running,
jumping and frolicking,
of a loved one, no longer there.

Half smiles,
nods and listens
to barks, yelps and whines
no one else can hear.

Gone are the licks on her hand,
the wag of an old dog's tail,
the warm body she carried
up and down the stairs.

Good memories do not
write themselves into a book,
nor are the best memorials
carved on a slab of stone.

ANCESTORS TAKE A WALK
BY RENATE HANCOCK

My grandfather came
from a place where
his native language was outlawed.
All would speak German,
or not speak at all.

My grandmother talked
from dawn through dusk,
a bubbly babble that was burst
in primary school, when someone said:
"Your mother left you, she didn't want you!"

Truth was outed.
Though
it didn't silence
my grandma for long.
Her bubble expanded and grew.

My grandparents met when she walked through
his freshly planted
potato field
in high heels.
An unwanted aeration.

But he loved her
for it
just the same.
They were servants
in a wealthy town
for a
judge's daughter, who
lived alone.

Miss Adelaide preferred
the company of women,
which wasn't allowed.

So she befriended
A man who sold
whiskey.

They never drank it,
but talked, in the library,
or walked
the grounds
my grandfather landscaped.

My grandmother scolded
Miss Adelaide.
"Live your life. It's the only one you'll get."

Miss Adelaide grew old and died,
rich and alone.
Lonely.
In a house with sixteen-foot ceilings
and thirty-six rooms.

My grandparents bought a farm,
and raised
two strong daughters.
I am their fifth grandchild.
The writer.

It is sad to think
that only because of me
will anyone remember
Miss Adelaide
at all.

But the man who planted
potatoes, and the woman
who trampled them in heels,
walk with me
every single day.

THE TRACKS WE LEAVE BEHIND
BY JACQUELINE CORLISS

Thistles in the threads of a child's sock.
The mother nailing footprints into lose earth.

The homeless man in a new tie
and someone's grandmother preaching
to a congregation of pigeons
wait beside the ghost of an old railroad station.

The young man crossing the street, saved
by one second, but he doesn't know.

The husband beside a hospital bed
dear, take me with you.
At home the last few leaves
hang from their branches, ready to fall.
In the tall green grass, two long tracks
from the wife's stretcher he refuses to mow.
Also, the calico on the front porch, waiting.
The silence of it all.

TO BE

BY SHEALA DAWN HENKE

Clear the white
Drifting
Time fleeting, precious and pure

Make way for the secrets
Of the New, unbound
And still lost to future's
Great frontier

And how we weave
The woolen overcoat of so many moments,
Tracings of thread so strong
As strong as stardust

Blow it to the wind,
And Life's melodious breeze
Can carry it back to you
And me,
To Be
Just Be

WHISPERS OF NICK
BY DEAN K MILLER

Wind riffles the lake
wrinkled lines racing toward shore
but the leaves on the trees
remain undisturbed.
I draw a breath–
Startled at breaking the silence.

How many have crossed
on my journey to reach this place?
A young man's soul follows my progress
watching from a distance–
uncertain. I wait as
wind riffles the lake.

I know he's here
can feel his energy nearby.
It's time for him to go
to heed his father's calling–
a love cry from the other side carried on
wrinkled lines racing toward shore.

I grasp at shadows
reaching for a life expired
if only to extend my own
and come up empty handed.
Everything here is dead
but the leaves on the trees.

Vibrant and green
except for one
that drops at my feet
crumbling in to dust–
like so many ashes to
remain undisturbed.

I cannot leave this place
not yet–not until I know
my reason for being here.
Seeing answers; finding questions;
dropping to my knees
I draw a breath

And hold it in
to know his last breath
letting go when I hear
a whispered voice
echo from the horizon
Startled at breaking the silence.

A TRIAD OF WAYS
BY BEN HUMPHREY

I'm on my way
the goal I can see

I tread the *Way*
I cannot know

It's the yin and yang
of making my way.

THERE IS PEACE

BY JUNE CAROLUS

peaks cascade across painted skies
as quilted mounds of patchwork blanket a masterpiece
sunbeams capture majestic reflections of
weather beaten accents molded from time
pine and aspen regenerate
boulders gravitate toward swollen streams
the howling of a wolf echoes across a ridge
slowly the sun is swallowed by shadows
carved from the creator of wind and rain
chipmunks scurry into claw made dug outs
as snowflakes glide and touch the ground
ice crystals form barriers to a once warm earth
elk retreat into a hibernating forest
paw prints indented in pyramids of snow
leave behind a captivating sight
all creatures sleep beneath an umbrella of mossy crevices
and there is peace

CONTRIBUTOR BIOGRAPHIES

Belle Schmidt: Canadian native, Belle Schmidt took up writing poetry after her retirement from business. She studied Journalism and Poetry at the University of Washington in Seattle. Her work has appeared in several anthologies, magazines, newspapers and on-line. Belle has published three chapbooks, *Do Carrots Cry, My Poems* and *Baubles & Bric-a-Brac*. Her collection of 101 poems is titled *Poems From my Pocket*. *In Our Bones,* her fifth book was released in December, 2015.

Ben Humphrey: In his not so wasted youth, Ben was a river rat, back packer, and skier. In retirement, he started writing poetry. *The Magpie Cried,* was published and he was named Colorado's Senior Poet Laureate in 2013. A collection of Taoist poems is the next project.

C. A. Strazer: C A. Strazer is a retired teacher, licensed counselor, health educator, and freelance writer. Four of her stories have been published in the *Chicken Soup for the Soul* series. Carol's articles and essays have appeared in *Woman's Day, The Power of Living, Christian Living in the Mature Years,* and regional publications. Her poems have been published in four anthologies. Carol's historical novel, *Barbed Wire and Daisies,* is based on the little-known World War II story about a German Christian family struggling to survive in refugee camps.

Dean K Miller: Dean is a freelance writer, professional member of Northern Colorado Writers, and Colorado Poets Center. His poetry has appeared in several print and online literary magazines. His first poetry book, *Echoes: Reflections Through Poetry and Verse* was published by Hot Chocolate Press in November 2014. He published his next poetry book, *Sometimes the Walls Cry: A Book of Haiku and Sketch*, via his own imprint. Miller, a high school soccer team mate of contributing photographer Scott Scofield, spends his spare time fly fishing. He lives in Colorado.

Dina Baird: Dina Baird is a writer, digital content marketing professional, ecologist, humanitarian, scientist, outdoor enthusiast, music lover, coffee and wine connoisseur, traveler, mother, friend and seeker.

Doris Miller: (no relation to Dean K Miller) Doris Miller is a mother of three, foster mom of 14, and caring mom for abused women who lived with us. She taught elementary school in IA, MN, and CA. Now retired in CO she is taking care of her Parkinson's-Dementia husband, writing poetry and her memoirs.

Eleanore D. Trupkiewicz: Eleanore D. Trupkiewicz, award-winning author and poet, has poems published in the 2012 anthology *Measuring Twine: Poetry With Strings Attached*. Her submission "Poetry by Keats" won the 2013 Writer's Digest Short Short Story Competition out of more than six thousand entries. She writes speculative fiction and provides editing, proofreading, and data entry services to a small clientele. Her other passion is helping others realize their potential, putting to work her varied interests in personal growth and psychology, color psychology, and fashion to do so. Eleanore works with gratitude out of her local Starbucks coffee shop. Find her online at http://refinersfireediting.com

Jacqueline Corliss: Jacqueline Corliss sparks the world as Yogi, daughter, sister, auntie, word girl, and POET. She lives in Fort Collins, CO with her beloved felines Inkspot and Wickham.

Jennifer J. Goble, Ph.D.: Jennifer, a psychotherapist living in Estes Park, Colorado, enjoys writing, drawing, and riding across America on a Polaris Spider. She is a contributing blogger of *The Writing Bug*, writes weekly newspaper columns about mental health, and writes rural women stories on her blog: www.ruralwomenstories.com. The author of *My Clients…My Teachers: The Noble Process of Psychotherapy*, Jennifer has a Ph.D. in Counseling Education from CSU. Women raised with only sisters, is the research within her dissertation. She writes poetry only while riding the city bus. Her anxiety relaxes, and secluded thoughts emerge while held captive in an environment of ever-changing diversity.

June M. Clymer: June M. Clymer is a writer of poetry and children's picture books. She holds an AA degree in Liberal Arts and is also a graduate of The Institute of Children's Literature. She is a member of the Society of Children's Book Writers & Illustrators (SCBWI), Northern Colorado Writers, and Front Range Christian Fiction Writers. Three of her poems have been published in the book Combat Trauma: The Spousal Response to PTSD. She is the author of A Journey to Publication and Beyond. She lives near the Rocky Mountains of Northern Colorado with her husband and three dogs.

Kari Redmond: Kari Redmond is an English as a Second Language teacher at Colorado State University. She is currently working on her first novel, *This Story Takes Place in a Bar,* which requires extensive research in various bars throughout the world. She also writes short stories and flash fiction. Her works have been published in *The Tulip Tree Review, Brilliant Flash Fiction,* and an anthology called *Stops Along the Way.* Aside from writing, her biggest passion is traveling. She has a goal of visiting every country in the world. Ecuador, this past summer, was her 51st country.

Kathryn Mattingly: Kathryn Mattingly is the author of literary suspense novels Benjamin, Journey, Olivia's Ghost, The Tutor (2017) and short story collection Fractured Hearts. She has won five awards for her fiction. Kathryn teaches creative writing at a local college and is the coordinator for the Northern Colorado Writers Top of the Mountain writing contest associated with the NCW conference. Aside from her six books with Winter Goose Publishing, Kathryn's work can be found in numerous small press anthologies and print magazines.

Contributor Biographies

Kerrie Flanagan: Kerrie Flanagan is a freelance writer, author and writing consultant. She is the co-author of *Beauty Surrounds Us* and *The Paths We Take*, two inspirational coffee-table books that reflect the power that comes from combining poetry and photography. www.KerrieFlanagan.com

Kristi Joy: Kristi Joy began writing poems spontaneously about ten years ago during a period of intense spiritual growth. While at work as a massage therapist, some unfamiliar phrases started going through her mind. When she got home she sat down and started writing and realized it was a poem. Over the next few days around fifteen poems came pouring out. She has continued writing over the years since - at a slower pace! Kristi writes poetry as a way to more deeply experience and digest life.

Laura Mahal: Laura Mahal is returning to writing after a long absence. Into her twenties, Laura wrote articles for various journals, including editing the student publication for the University of Maryland's Augsburg (Germany) campus and a yearly newsletter for her fellow MP's from Fort McClellan. Laura specializes in literary fiction, with a completed novel and a handful of short stories and flash fiction in her portfolio. Her favorite daily practice is when she pens an email or a letter to a friend or colleague. "If my heart is involved, then I trust that my writing will advance, while remaining true to life."

Lorrie Wolfe: Lorrie Wolfe has been a poet all her life. She is passionate about the power of words to unite and move people. Her first chapbook of poetry and prose, Holding: from Shtetl to Santa, was published in 2013 by Green Fuse Press. Her work has appeared in Earth's Daughters, Progenitor Journal, Tulip Tree Review, Pilgrimage and Pooled Ink. Lorrie was named Poet of the Year at Denver's Ziggie's Poetry Festival for 2014-15. She is a technical writer and editor living in Windsor. Her business, Wolfe Unlimited, also provides grant writing and consulting in organizational development.

Monica Yoknis: Writing poetry has gotten Monica through some of her deepest bouts of depression. Mostly, she reads and writes mystery and supernatural thriller stories. Monica self-published her first novel, *Fear and Terror Stalk the Museum: An Artemis Lewis Adventure,* in

August 2016. She has developed a strange ability to turn string into things, usually with a crochet hook, but also dabbles with knitting needles. Her only "child" is a bunny named Peaches who is her rock of salvation; Monica adopted her, but Peaches rescued Monica. And speaking of rocks, Yoknis also collects fluorescent minerals.

Nancy L. Reed: Love of the written word inspired Nan to write from an early age: short stories, novels, memory snippets, scripts, and poetry. She calls Colorado the perfect place to live and is Musing at nancylreed.com about writing and designing a tiny house specifically for a wordsmith. She finds fellow writers excellent company and encourages everyone with a story or poem to put pen to paper.

Pam Wolf: Pam Wolf is a writer and poet who retired with her husband to an urban farm in Fort Collins in 2007. A volunteer and supporter of the Fort Collins Cat Rescue & Spay Neuter Clinic she is committed to animal welfare. Her book about Jake the therapy cat, who was the Shelter cat for the cat rescue was published in 2015. She is retired from the Presbyterian Church USA and served churches in Denver and Brighton. She continues to write poetry and thanks the Northern Colorado Writers for their dedicated support.

Patricia Walker: Patricia Walker, certified trainer/trailblazer for Infinite Possibilities, and Local Chapter Network Leader for The Monroe Institute, is the author of the award-winning body/mind/spirit memoir, Dance of the Electric Hummingbird, which is personally endorsed by rock legend Sammy Hagar. Patricia's articles and poems have appeared in The Loveland Reporter-Herald, Asana Journal, Aquarius Magazine, Elephant Journal, Los Cabos Magazine, and many more. She's currently working on her next book, along with furthering her studies in the field of human consciousness and is passionate about helping others discover their paths to self-realization. She's a member of Northern Colorado Writers and CIPA.

Renate Hancock: The mother of four survivors of middle school, Renate Hancock is passionate about the power of the written word. She works as the librarian at an elementary school, writes poetry and creative non-fiction, but considers herself primarily a novelist. Inspired by family and nature, she writes at the base of fourteen-thousand foot peaks and spends as much time as possible in the mountains and in her gardens.

S. E. Reichert: S. E. Reichert has been writing fiction, poetry, and essays for over twenty-five years. Her first paranormal romance series (*Fixing Destiny, Finding Destiny,*) will be completed this fall with its final installment (*Fighting Destiny*). Her poetry has been featured by Haunted Waters Press and TulipTree Publishing. She also contributes to the Be True, Be Love Website and is currently working on a new anthology of poems as well as a new series set in her home state of Wyoming.

Scott Scofield: (cover photographer) Scott Scofield is a retired U.S. Navy veteran, committed outdoorsman and photographer. "To experience nature is life-altering, to photograph nature is humbling." He currently resides in the Pacific North West.

Sheala Dawn Henke: Sheala has been an educator in the Poudre School District at Bennett Elementary, an I.B. World School for over seventeen years. Working closely with students and developing relationships with aspiring young writers has served as a direct line from her role as mentor to the muse. An active member of Northern Colorado Writers for over five years, her writing credits include 2016 title winning recipient of the Jerry Eckert Scholarship for philanthropic writers and hosting a successful crowdfunding campaign to independently publish her debut YA Science-Fiction series *IDEA33*. Sheala lives with her husband and two children in Fort Collins, Colorado.

Shelley Widhalm: Shelley Widhalm, who lives in Northern Colorado, is a journalist by day who writes poetry, short stories and novels and dabbles in drawing and painting. To learn more about her writing life, visit her website at www.shelleywidhalm. You can read her blog at shelleywidhalm.wordpress.com and her dog Zoey's blog at zoeyspaw.wordpress.com.

Summer Robidoux: Summer Robidoux graduated from Northwest Missouri State University with a BS in psychology/biology and received her DC from Cleveland Chiropractic College. She lives in northern Colorado with her husband and three young daughters. She likes to hike, ski, play volleyball, and write. Her novels include *The Pull* and *Finding Love Between the Lines*. You can find more about her at SummerRobidoux.com.

Zachary Gilbert: Zachary Gilbert is a Fort Collins born poet. He wooed his wife of 12 years with a fantastical 40 pages of rhymed verse, and silly cartoons. In the early 2000's he aspired to be a 3D animator as was professionally trained in creative writing and character development. He graduated from Front Range Community College in 2012 with an Associate of Science degree. Now he lives in Loveland with his wife and three kids and his dog Charlie. He loves to write whenever time allows. This book holds the first printed opportunity of his poetry to be available for public enjoyment.

ACKNOWLEDGMENTS

First and foremost, thanks to the poets of Northern Colorado Writers who answered the call for submissions. Without your courage to not only write the poems, but make them available for public reading, this book would be nothing but blank pages.

In January of 2016 I pitched the idea of an NCW Poetry Anthology to Director April Moore. Her response was an immediate "Go for it!" All of us in NCW are grateful for her support of our first poetry anthology.

To Jennifer Top of Tulip Tree Publishing, for your cover layout and design. You blended my desires with a photograph to create a wonderful piece of art for our cover.

Speaking of photographs, thanks to Scott Scofield for getting up so early to take the stunning picture used for the cover. I look forward to further collaborations in the future.

Finally, thanks to you, the reader (and supporter,) of all forms of poetry. The willingness to journey alongside the poet is an adventure not to be taken lightly. Your companionship on our travels is much appreciated.

ABOUT NORTHERN COLORADO WRITERS

Since 2007, Northern Colorado Writers has provided support and encouragement to writers of all levels and genres in NorthernColorado and beyond. Through monthly meetings, classes, networking, social events, our annual conference, our monthly newsletter, and our annual retreat, NCW helps writers navigate their way to success.

Our mission is to create a community where writers can inspire one another. NCW is composed of novelists, journalists, memoirists, poets, screenwriters, bloggers, children's book writers, and many more. We embrace diversity of gender, sexual orientation, and race, as we believe our individual backgrounds, perspectives, and passions help us create the stories we tell. We invite you to become a member of our community as you pursue your personal literary goals.

Learn more at www.NorthernColoradoWriters.com.

OTHER BOOKS IN THE NORTHERN COLORADO WRITERS ANTHOLOGY SERIES

Rise: An Anthology of Change

Published in 2019

www.ingramcontent.com/pod-product-compliance
Lightning Source LLC
Chambersburg PA
CBHW021954290426
44108CB00012B/1061